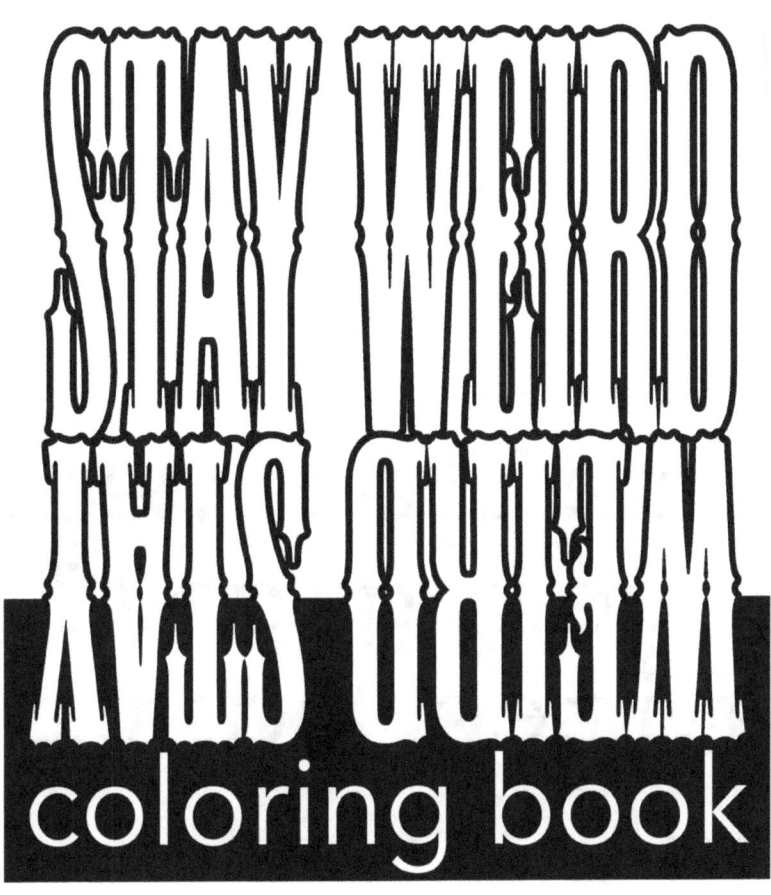

kate blume

ISBN: 978-0-6480847-4-7paperback.
BIC Subject category: 1. Drawing-coloring books for grown-ups 2. Arts & Photography- techniques
3. Craft, hobbies- art 4. Self-help-art therapy & relaxation 5. Self-help-anger management. 6.Self-help-stress relief

being called weird is
like being called a
limited edition

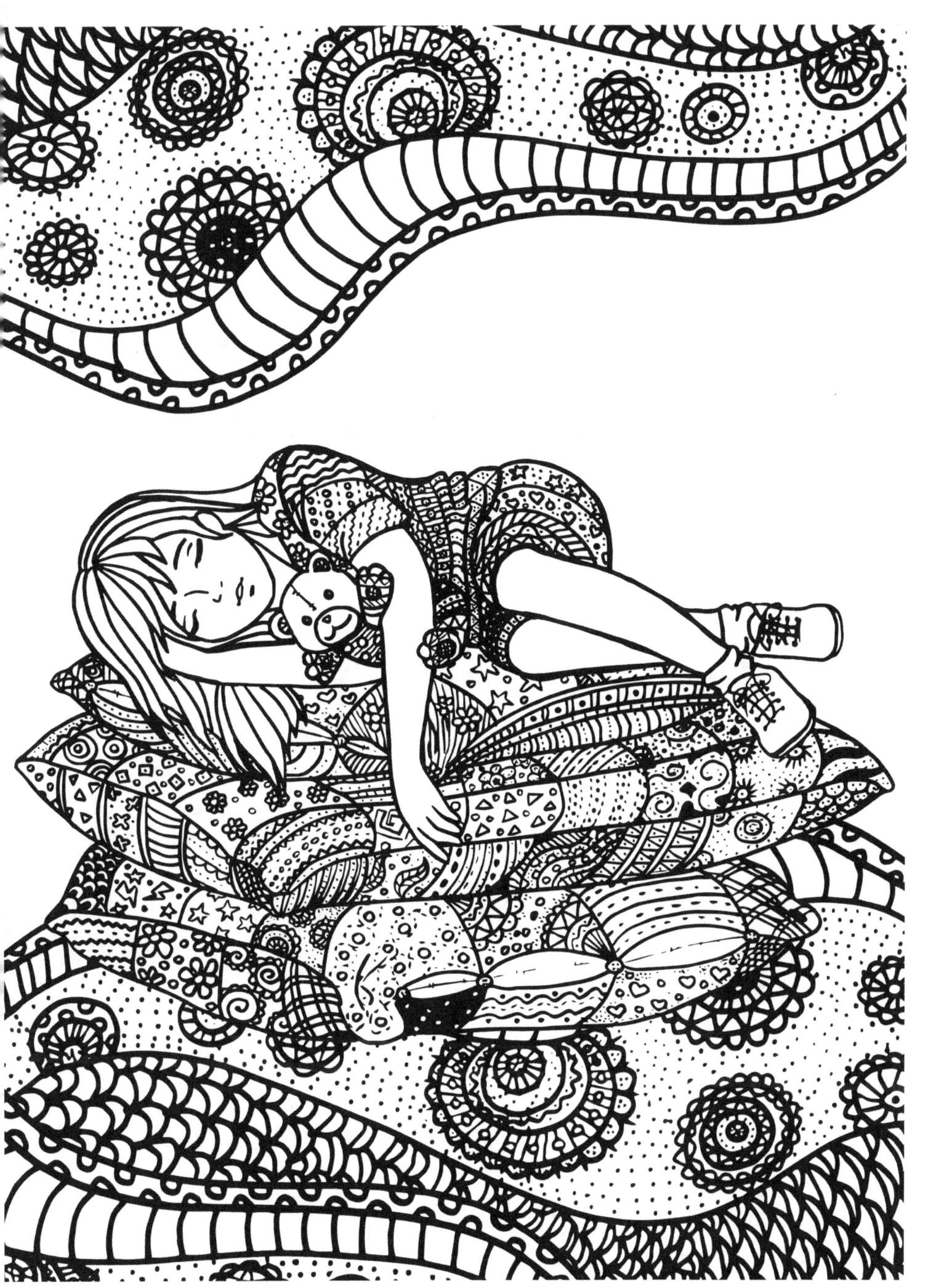

don't look for normal,
look for weird

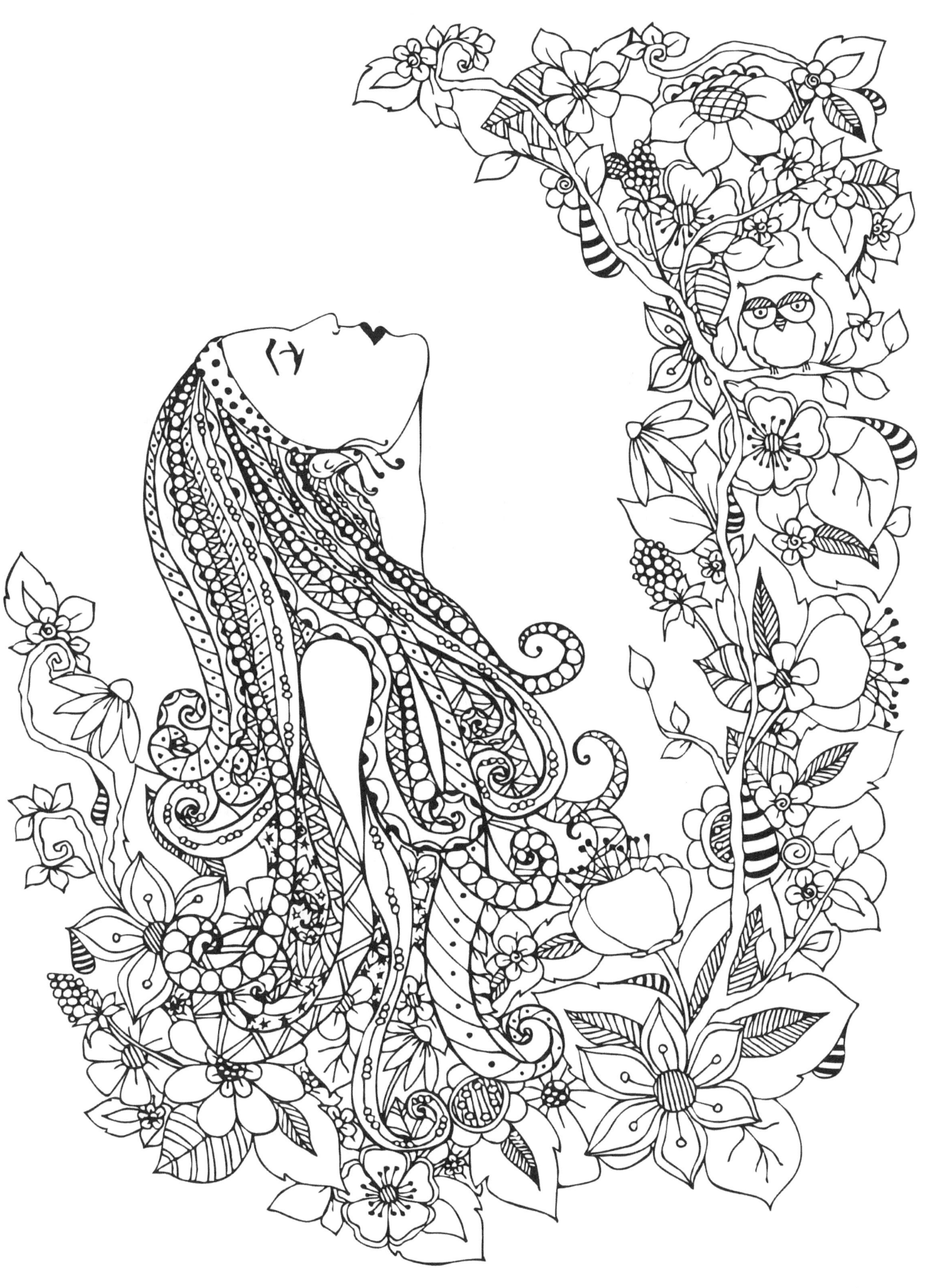

it's up to you to find
weirdness in the
normalist of days

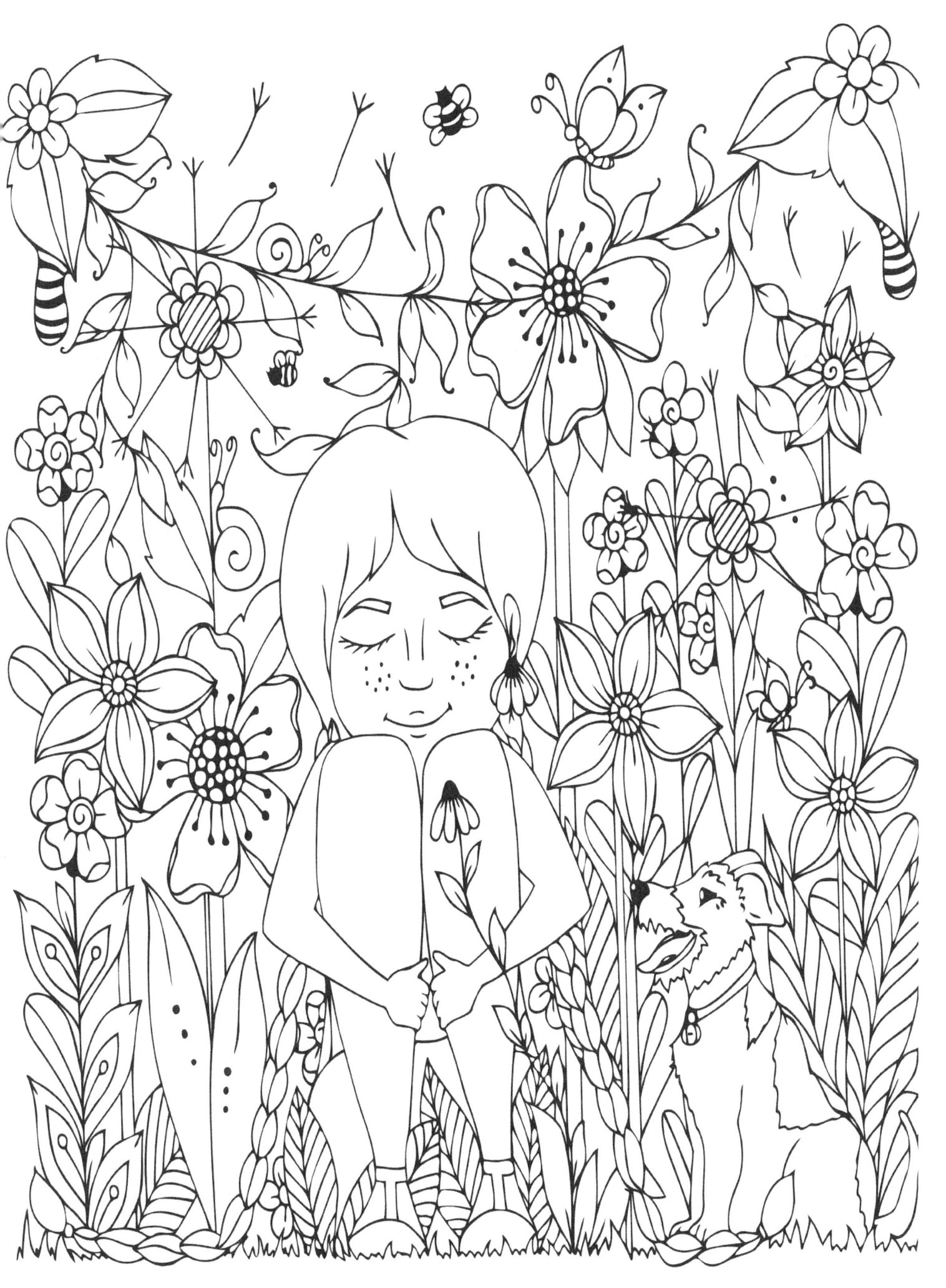

oh no! not you again

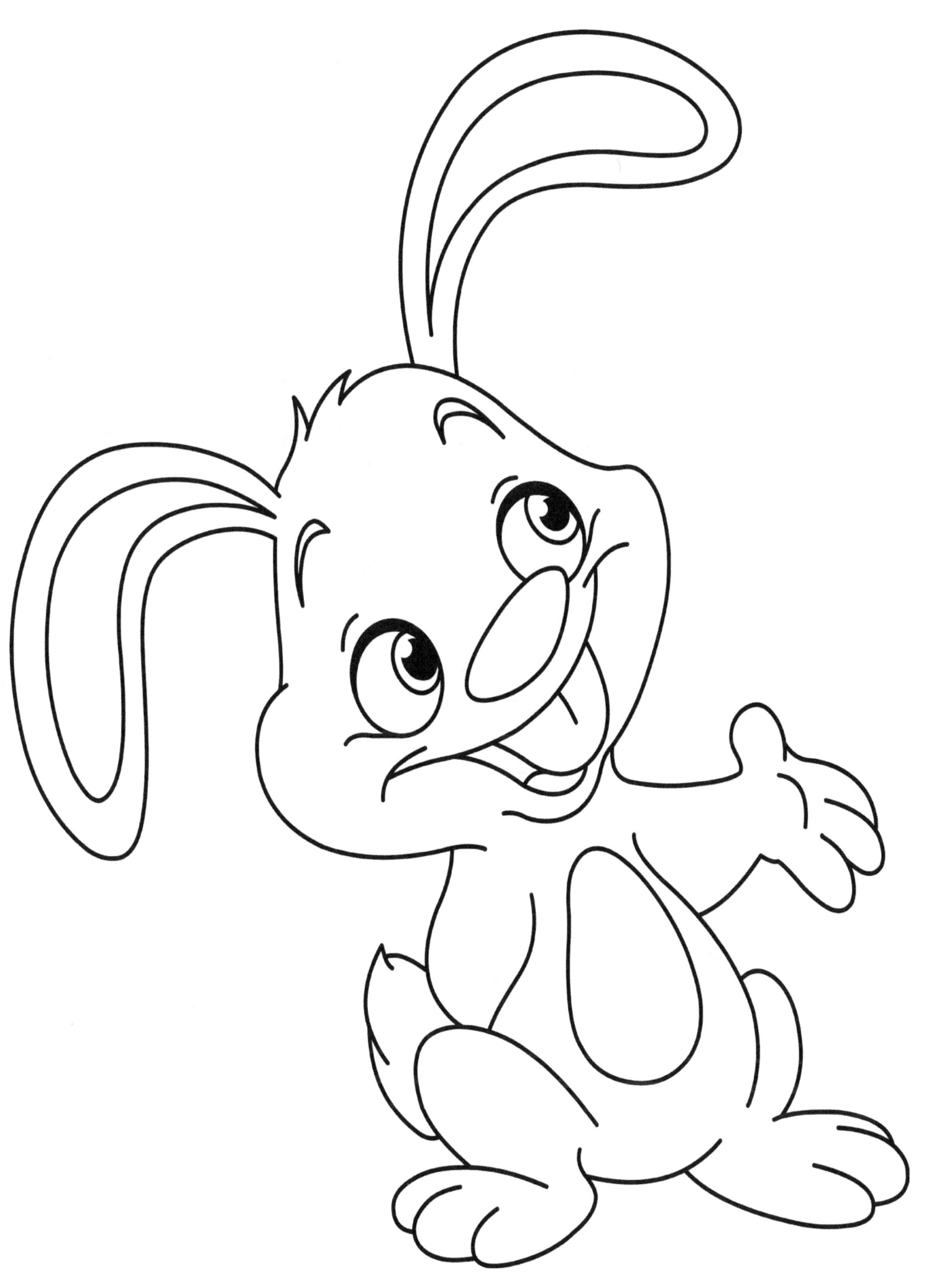

life is too short to be
normal, stay weird

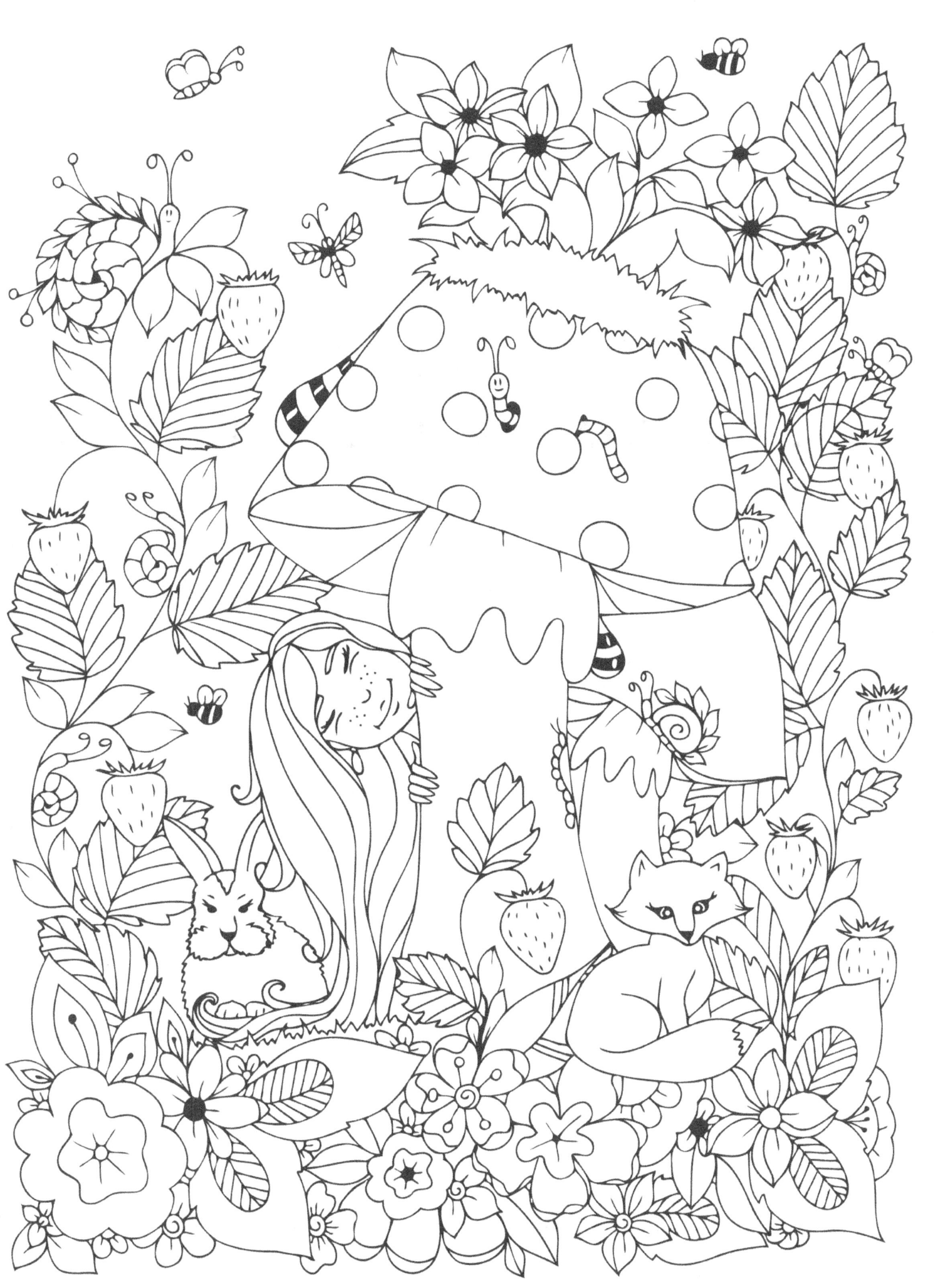

stay weird*
*i like you that way

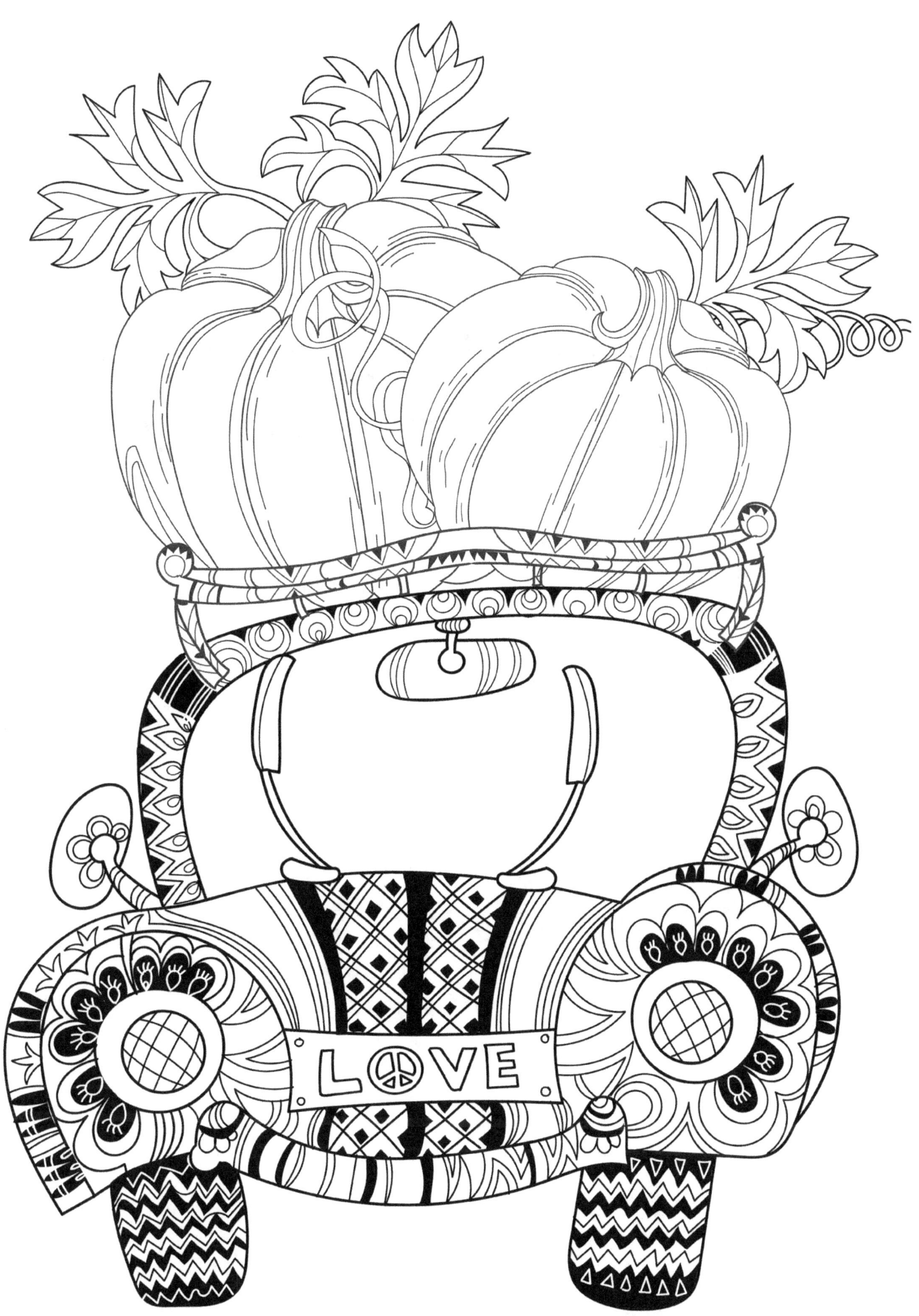

you are the perfect
type of weird

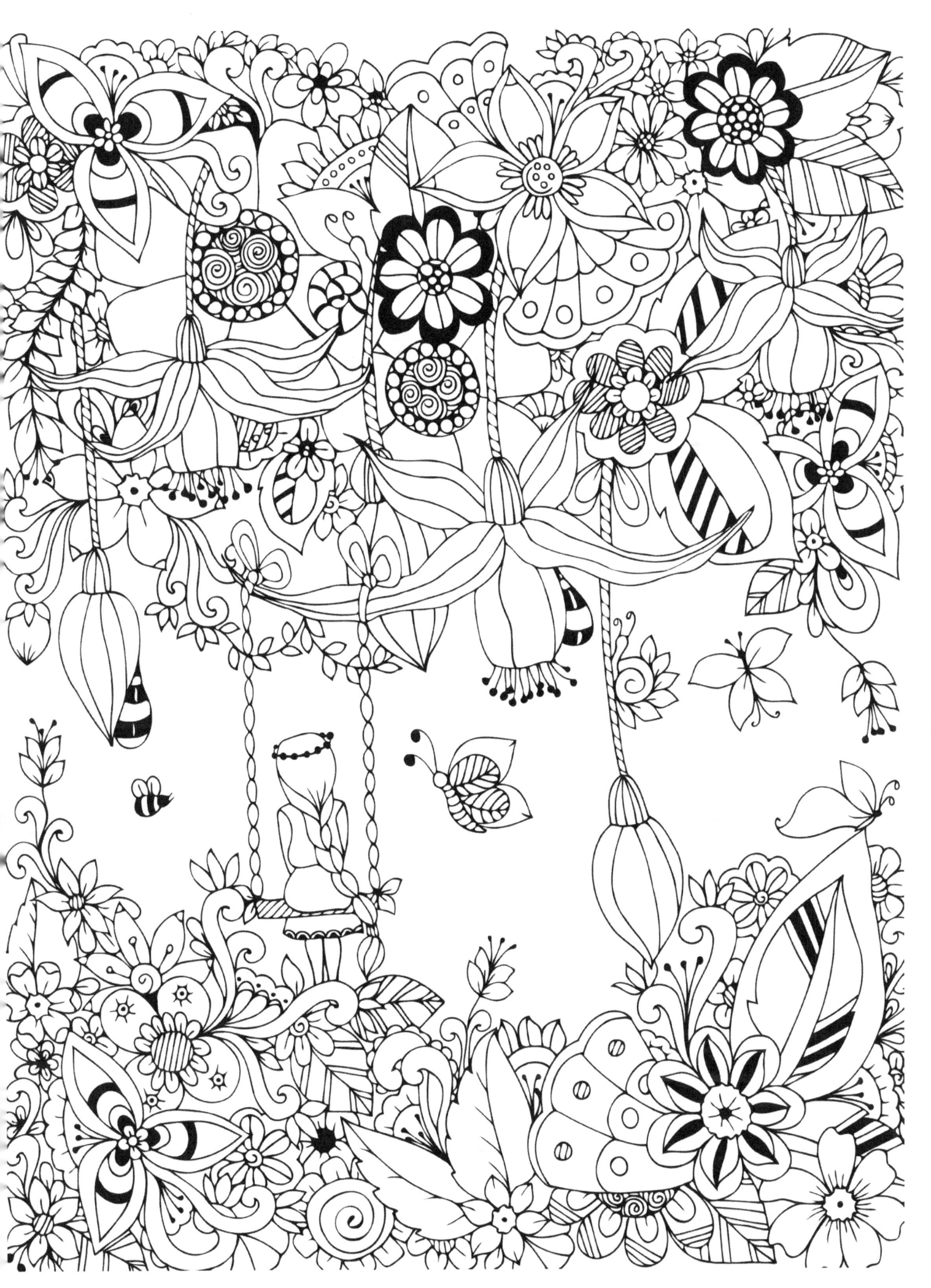

always be yourself, no
one does it better

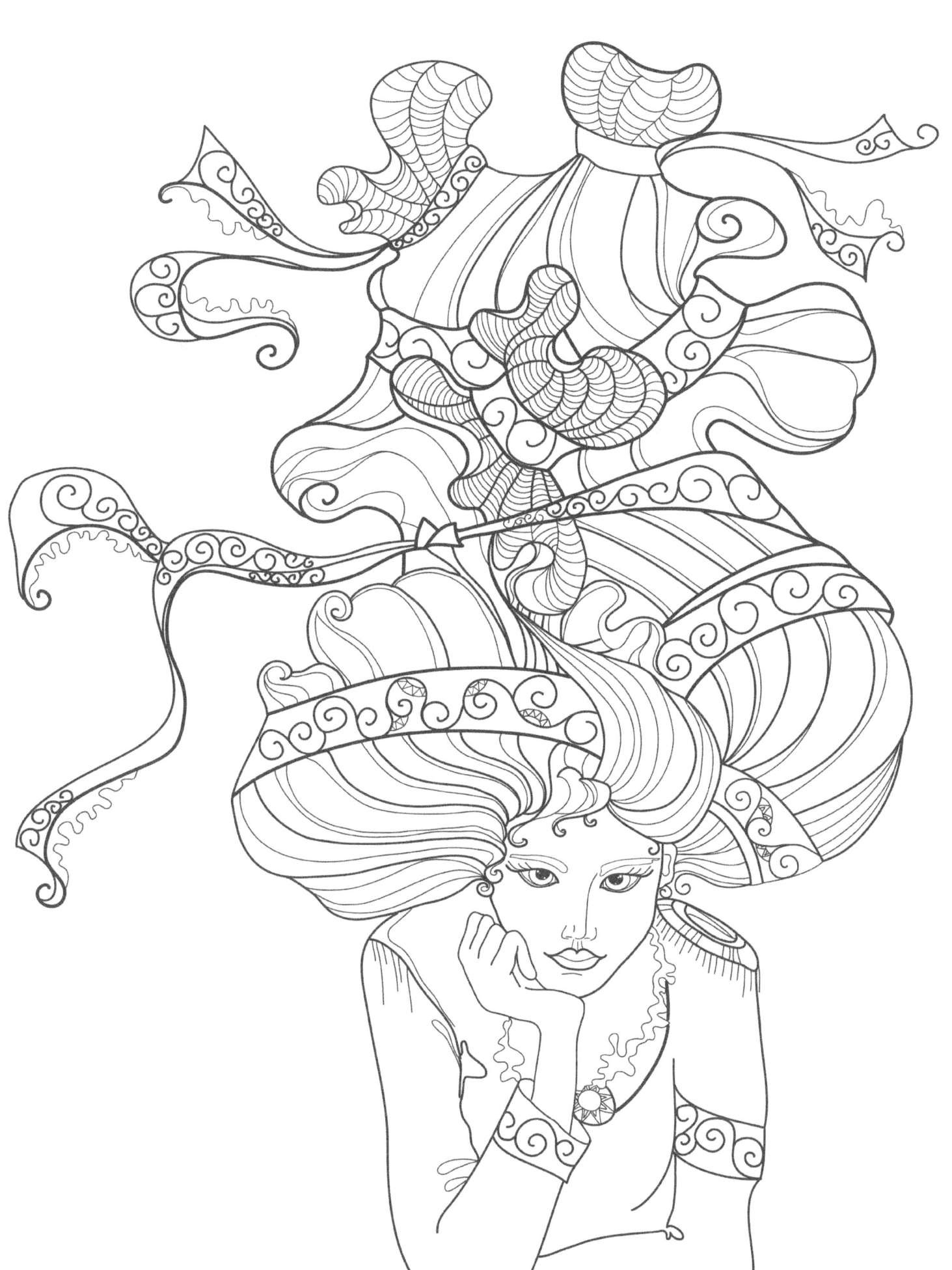

i'm not anti-normal,
i'm just pro-me

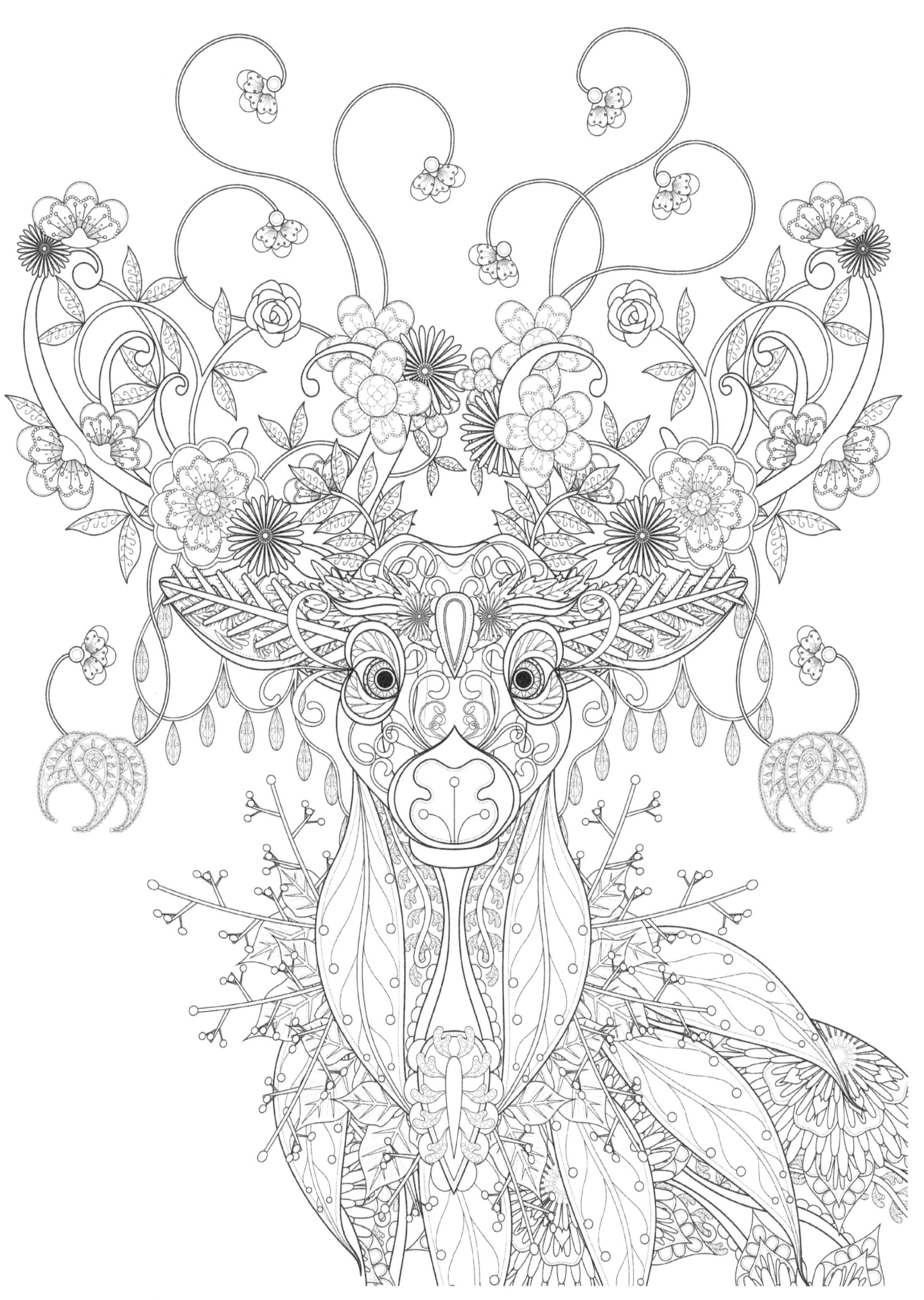

i hope you find it,
some day,
whatever it is

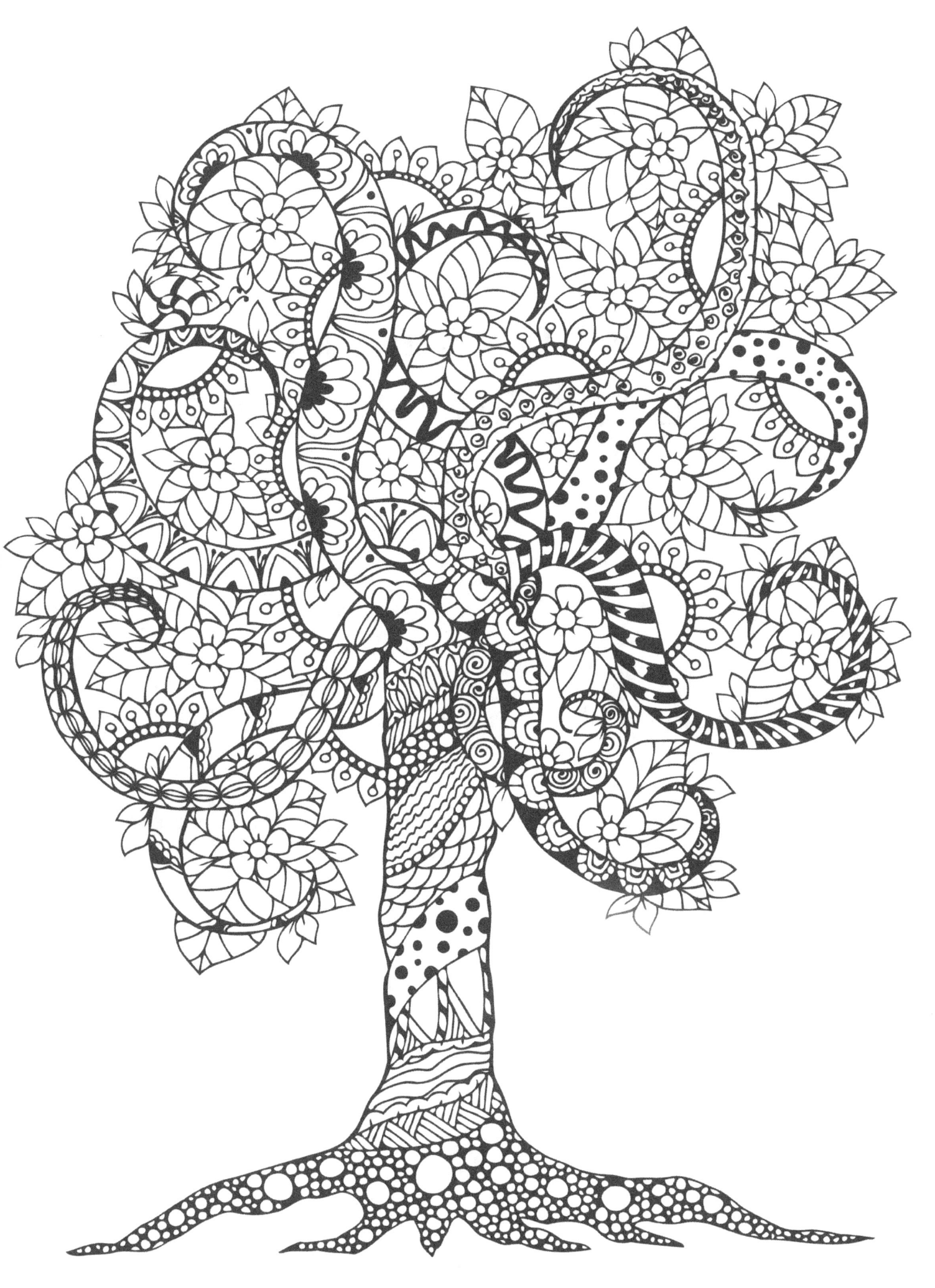

who am i?
that's secret

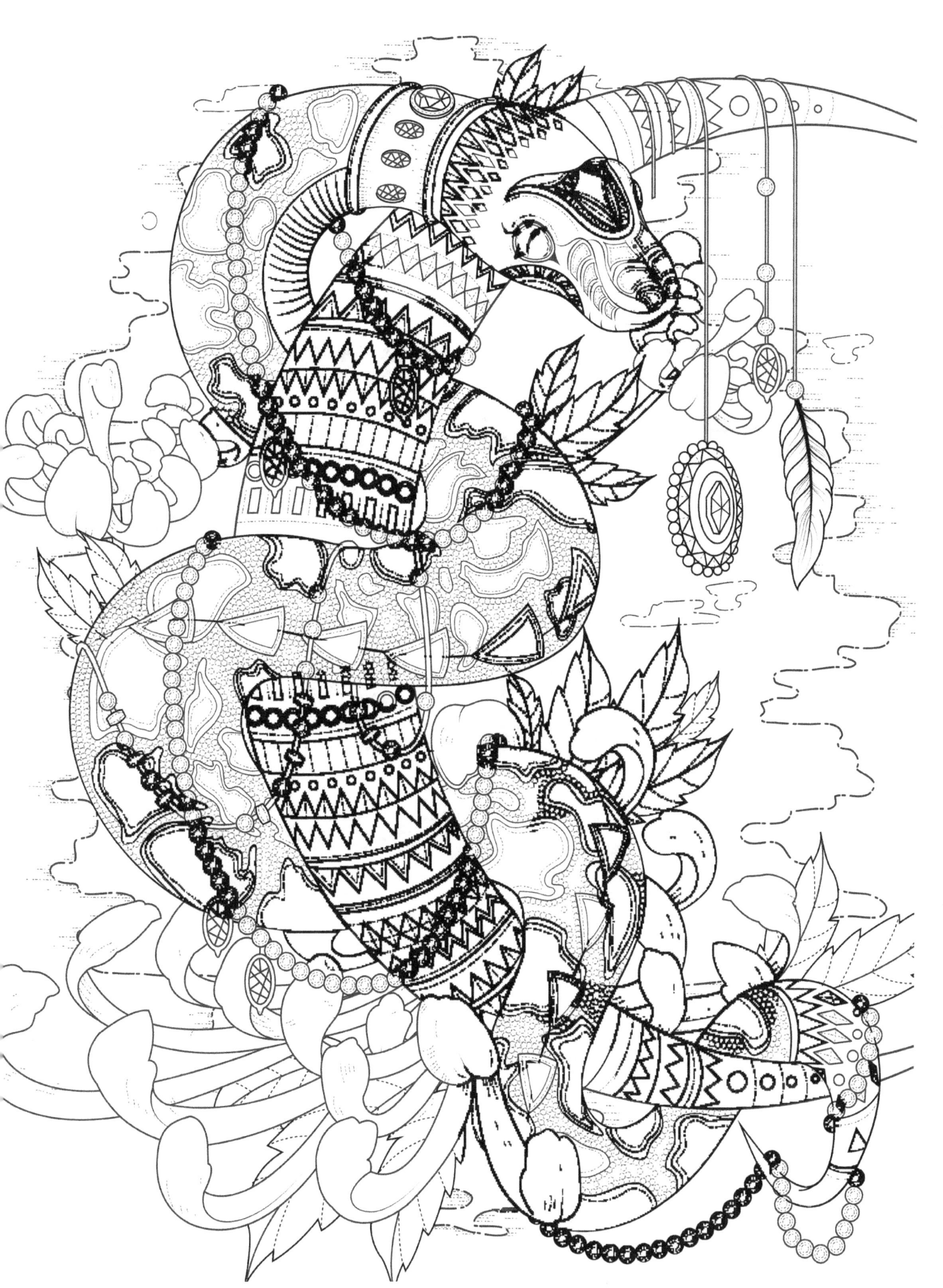

whatever makes you
weird and crazy,
that's your strength

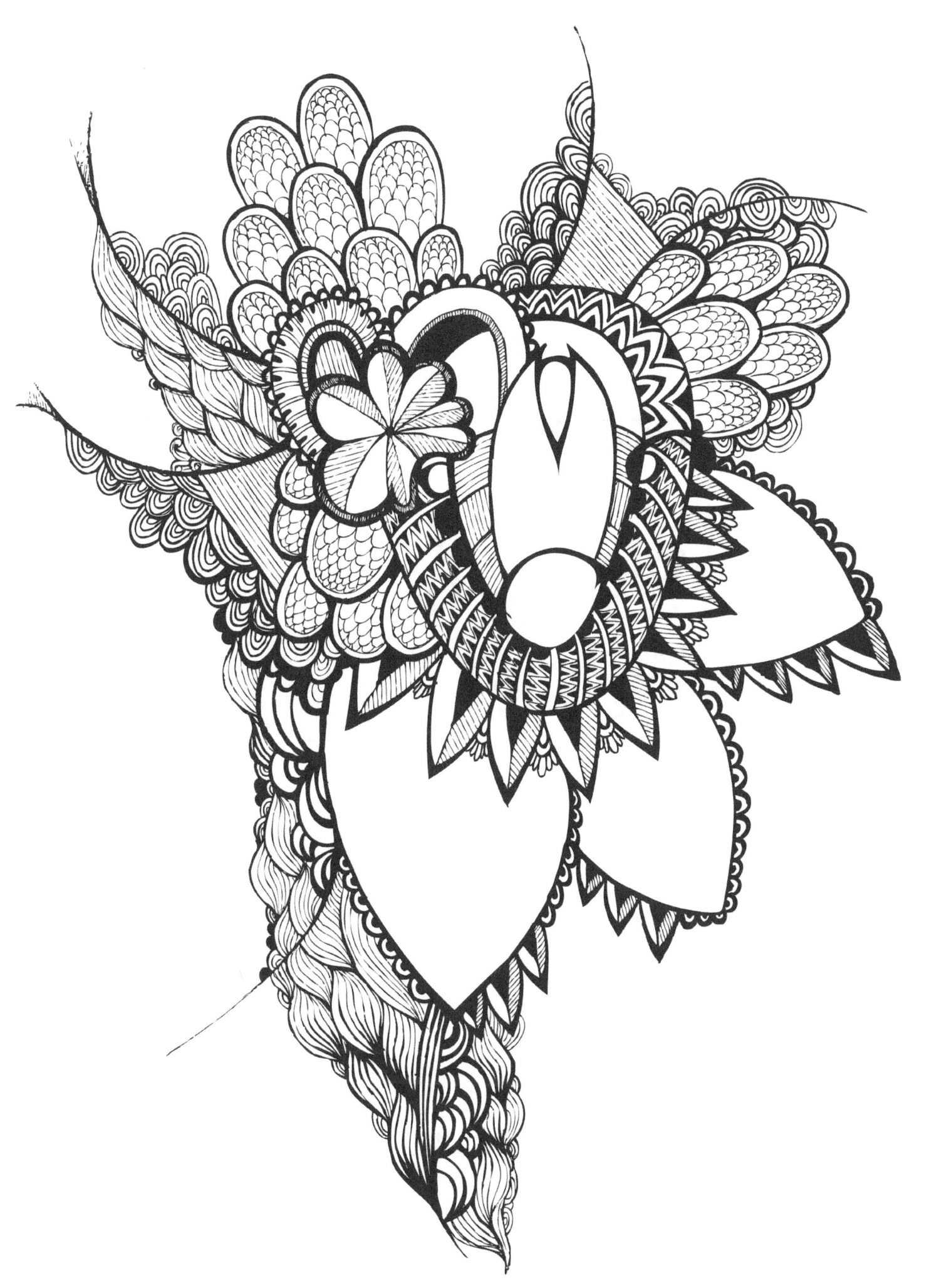

the more weird you are
the more fun you are

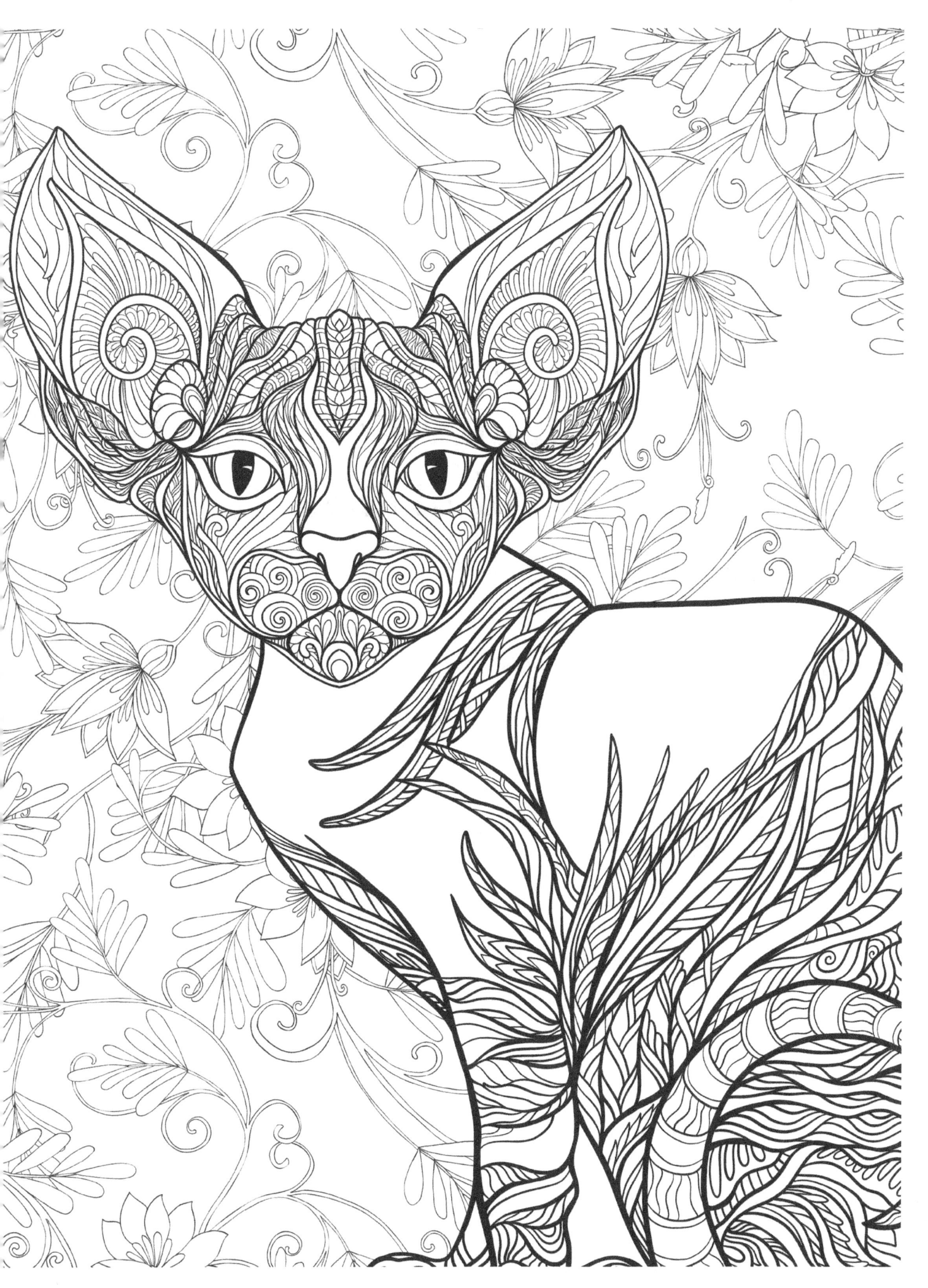

don't be afraid of being different, be afraid of being the same as everyone else

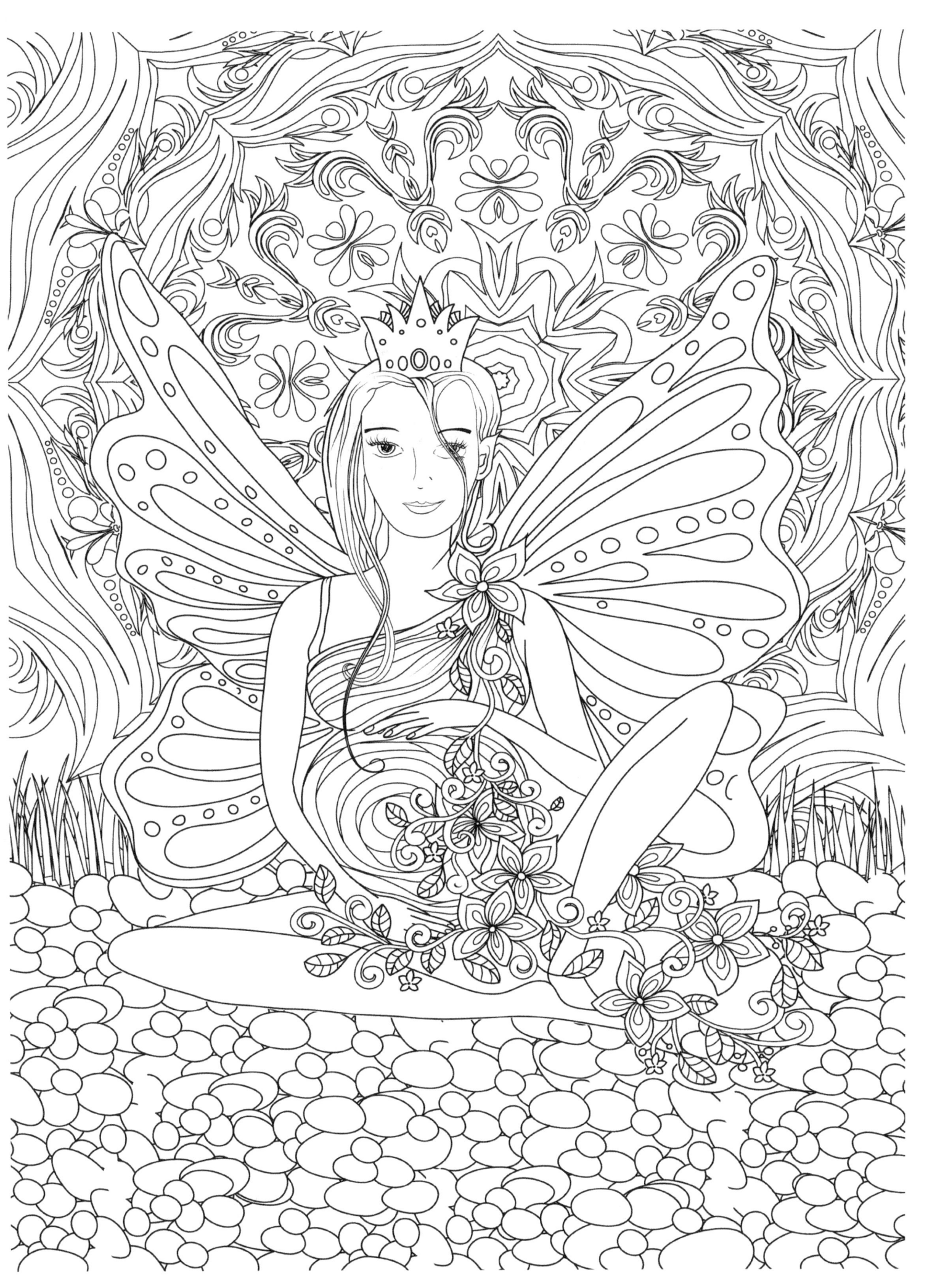

don't forget to be
awesome

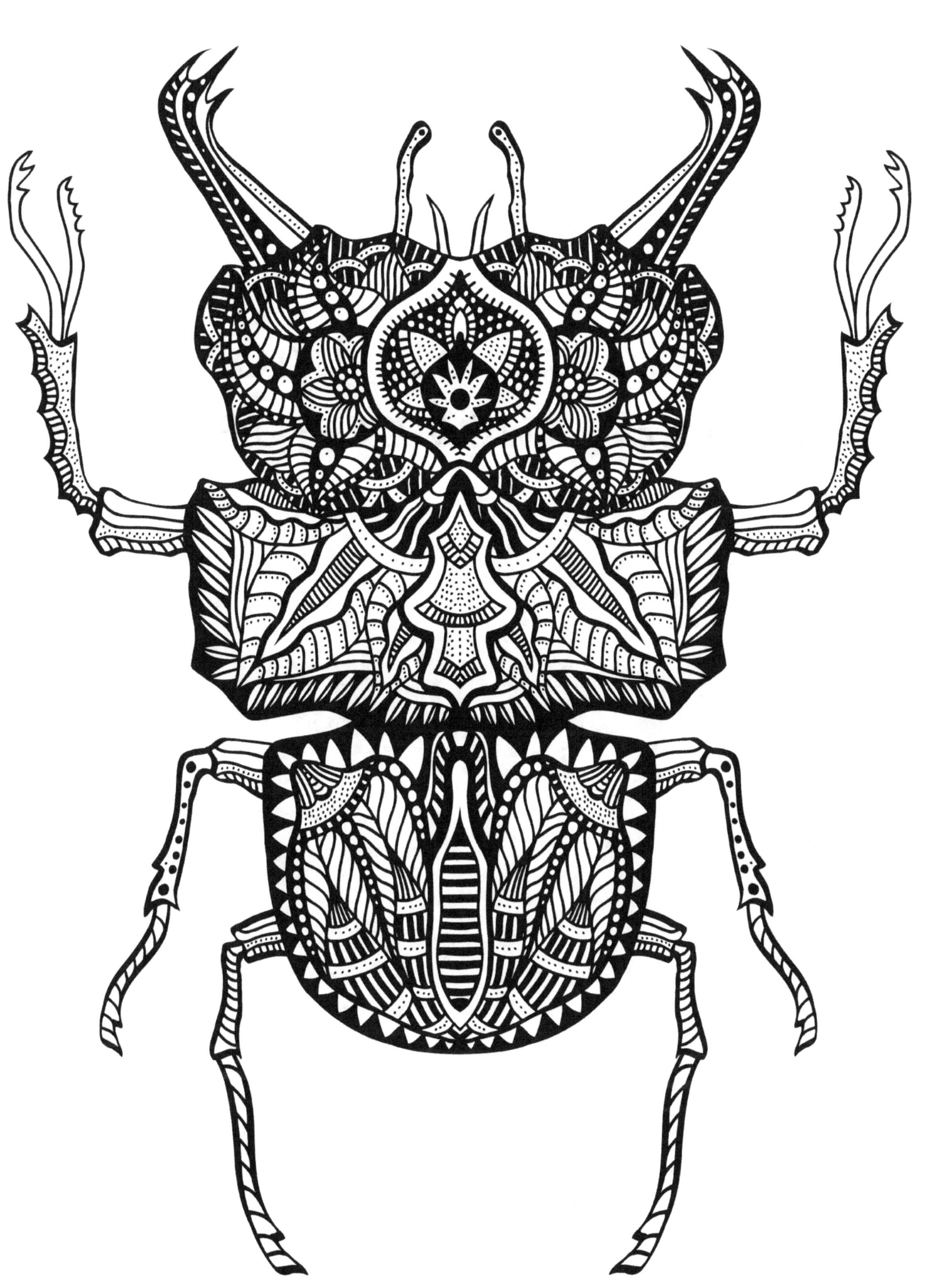

be one of those
regular weird people

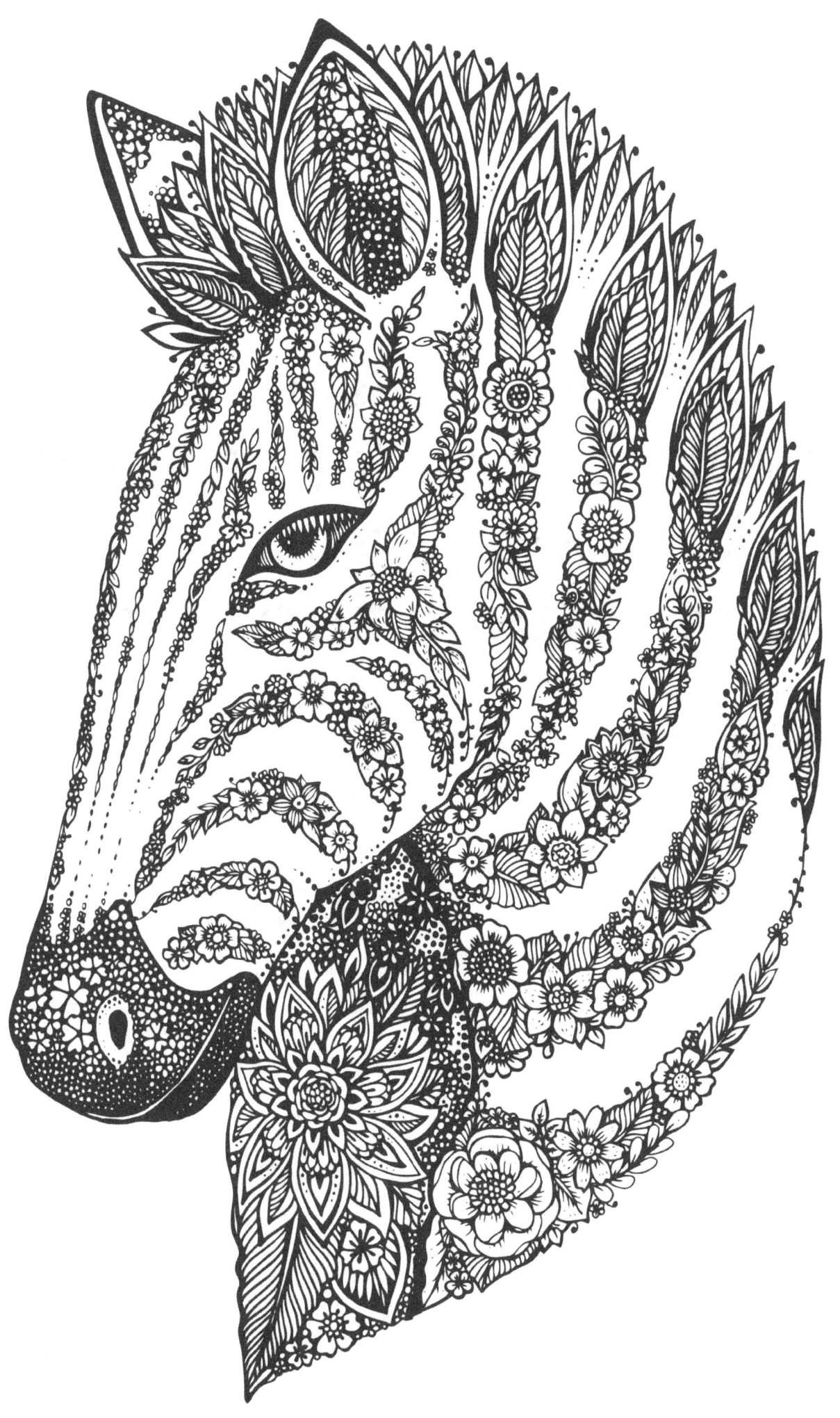

if you have the
power to make someone
feel good, you should
make them feel good

there is no
difference between who
i am and what i show

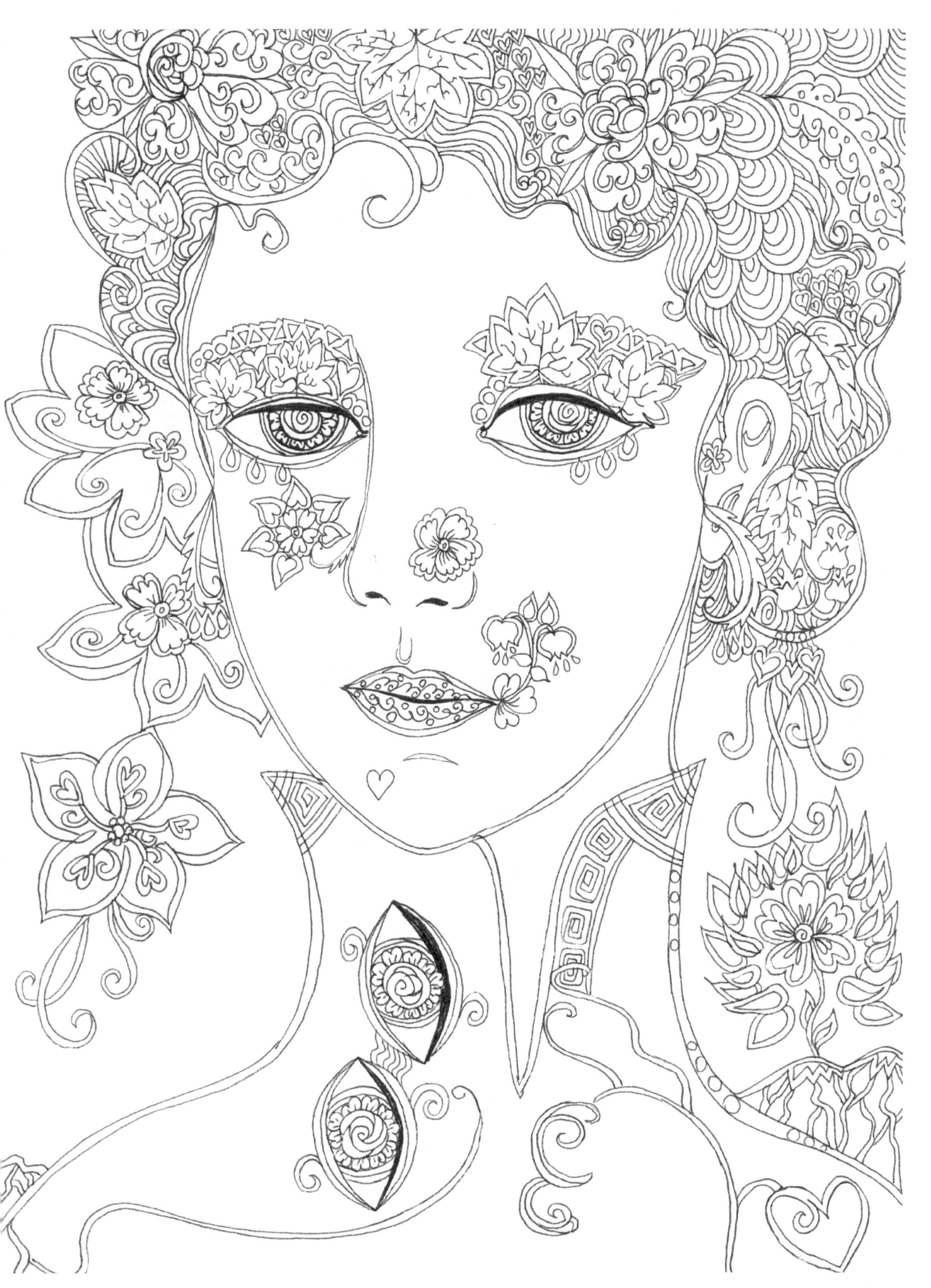

you're weird,
i like you

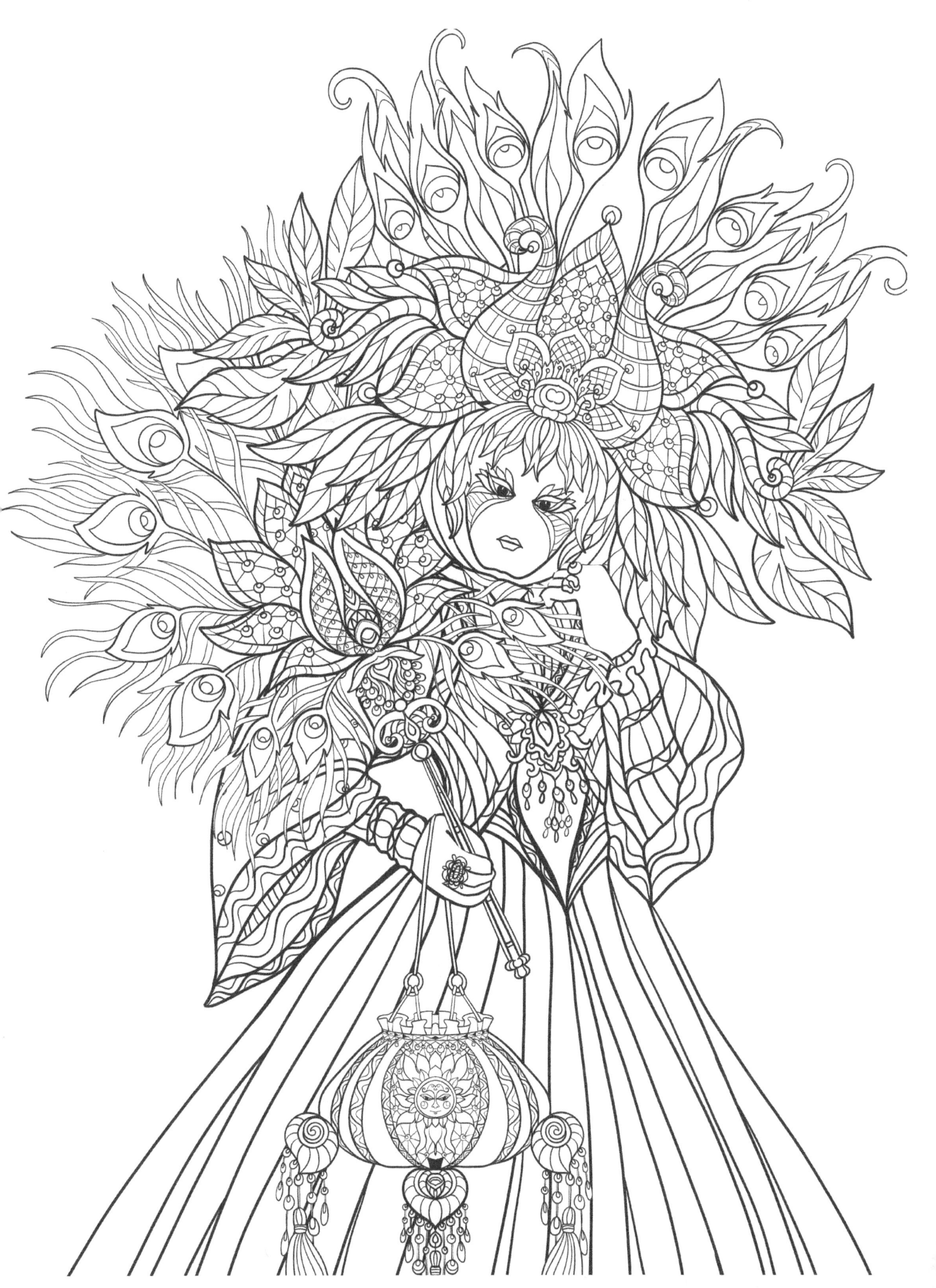

i like you because you
join in
on my weirdness

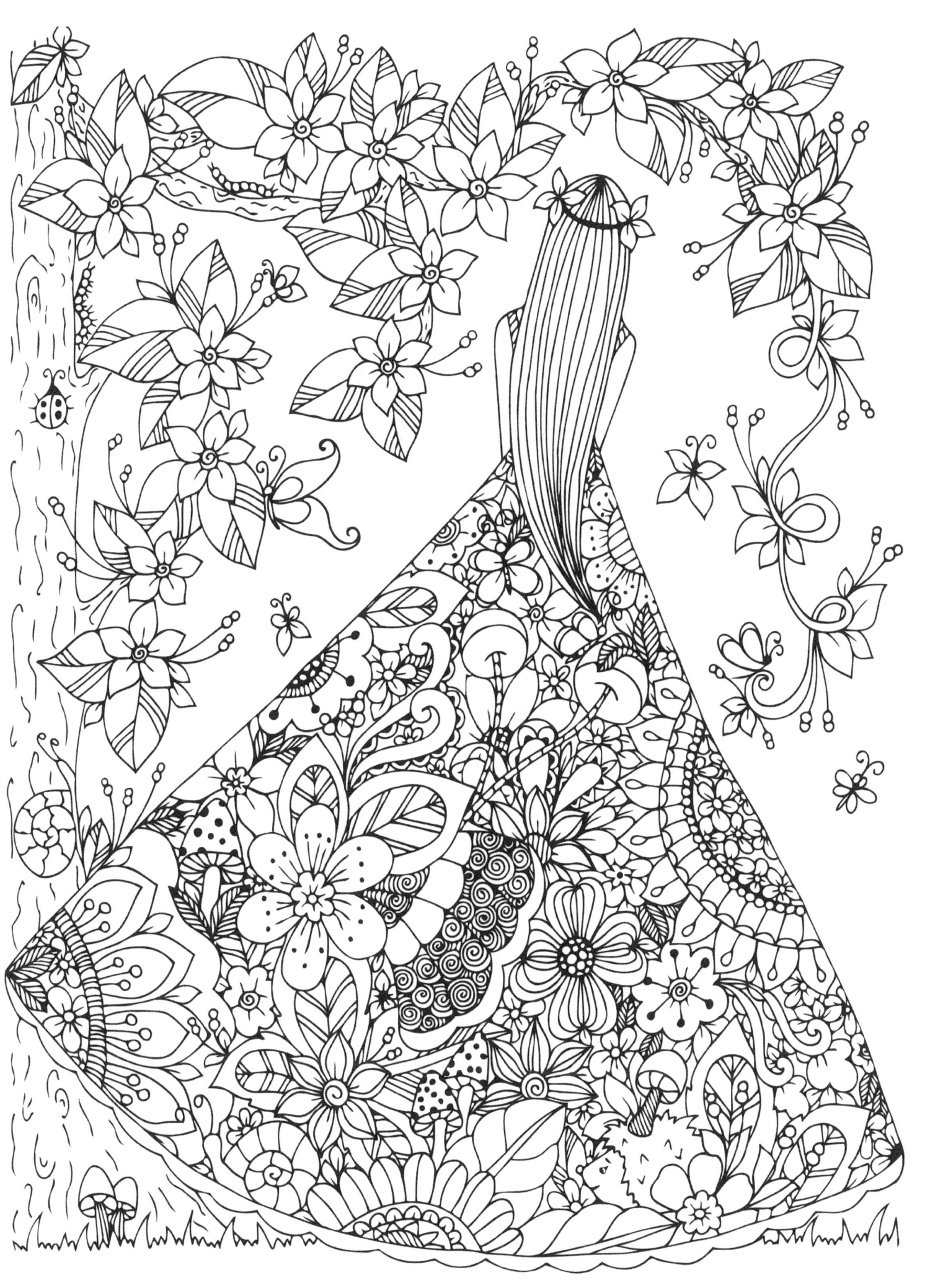

perfect is perfectly
boring

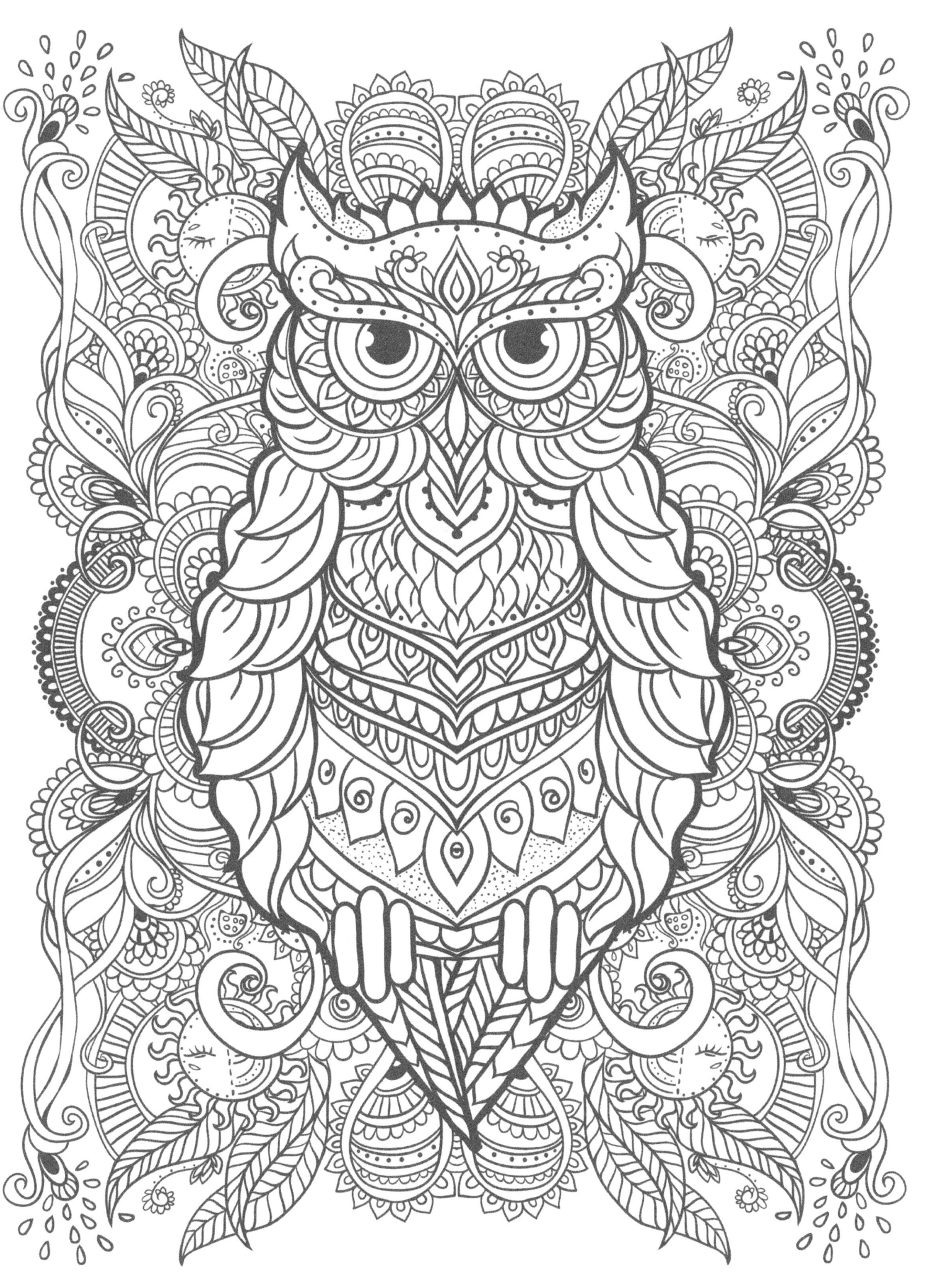

be happy,
be bright, be you

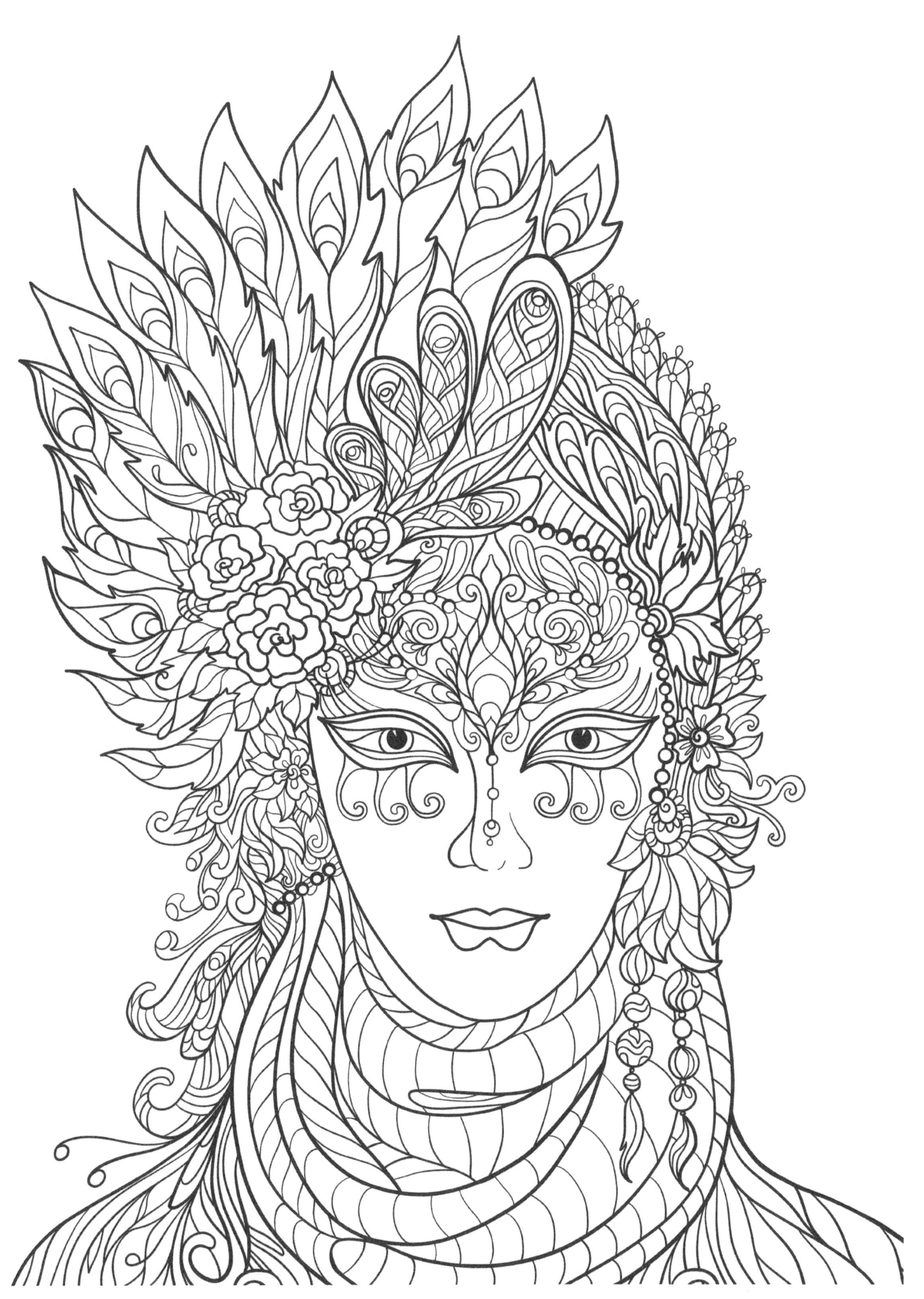

whatever, stay weird

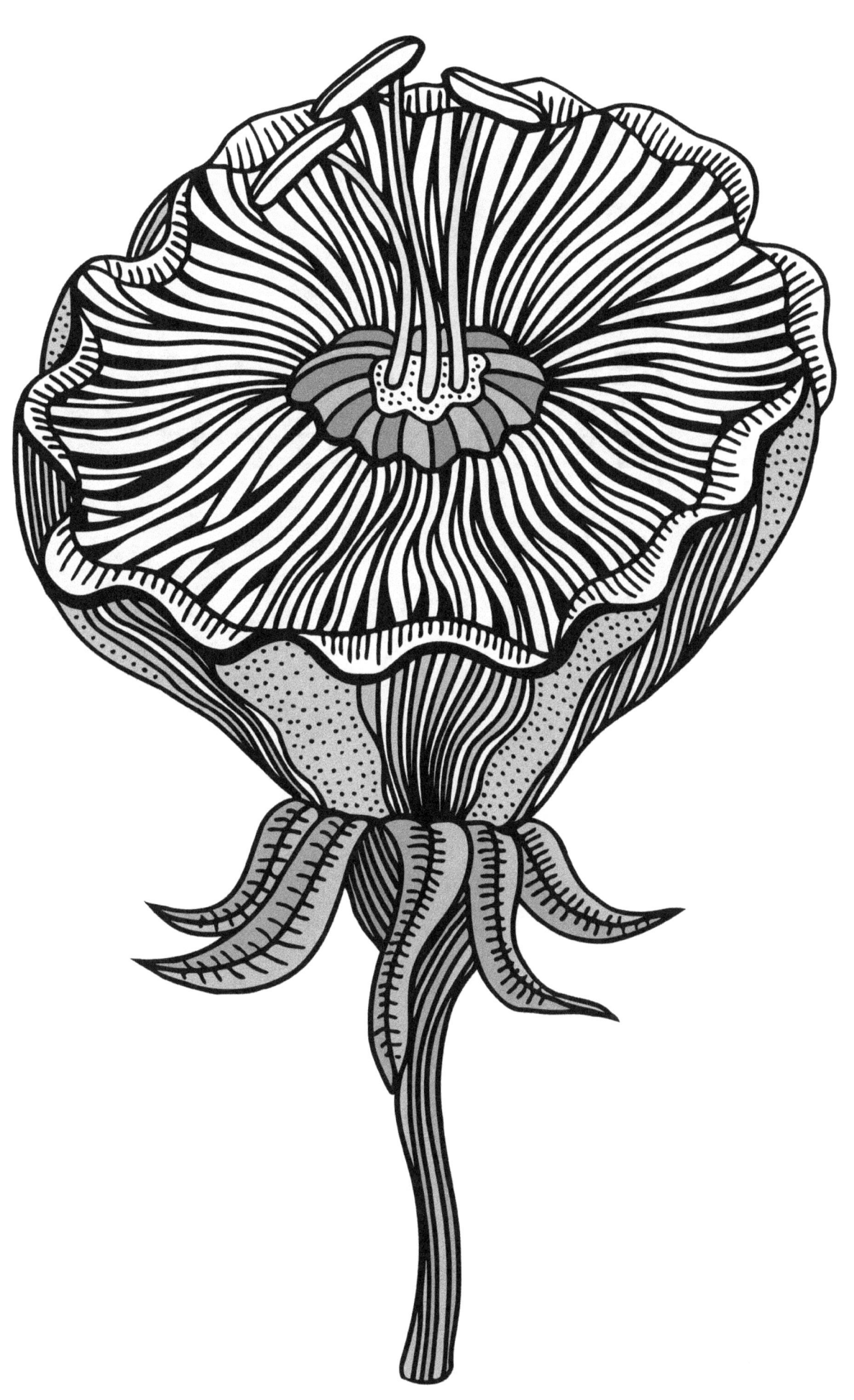

bee different
stay weird

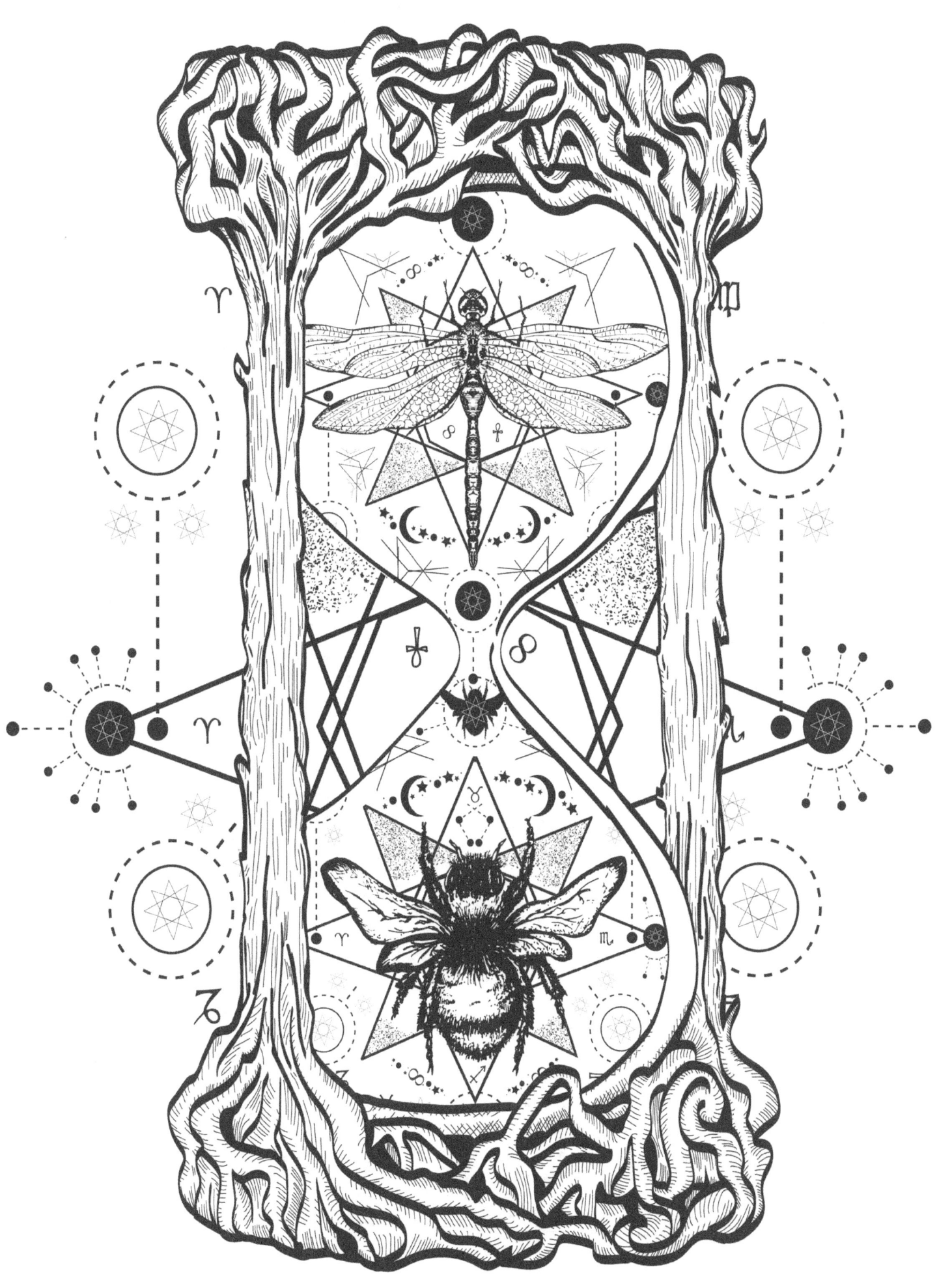

normal people worry me

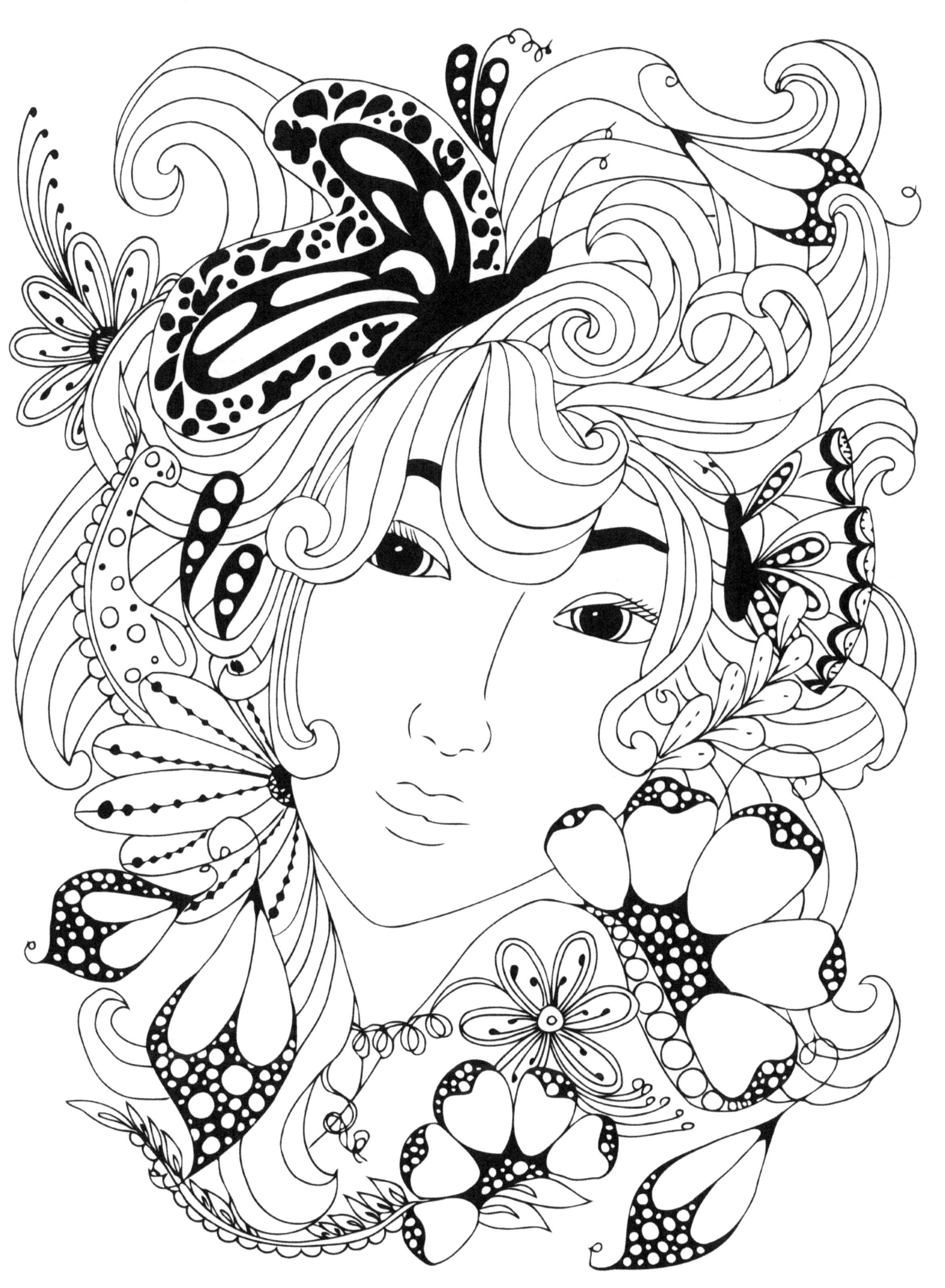

stay weird forever

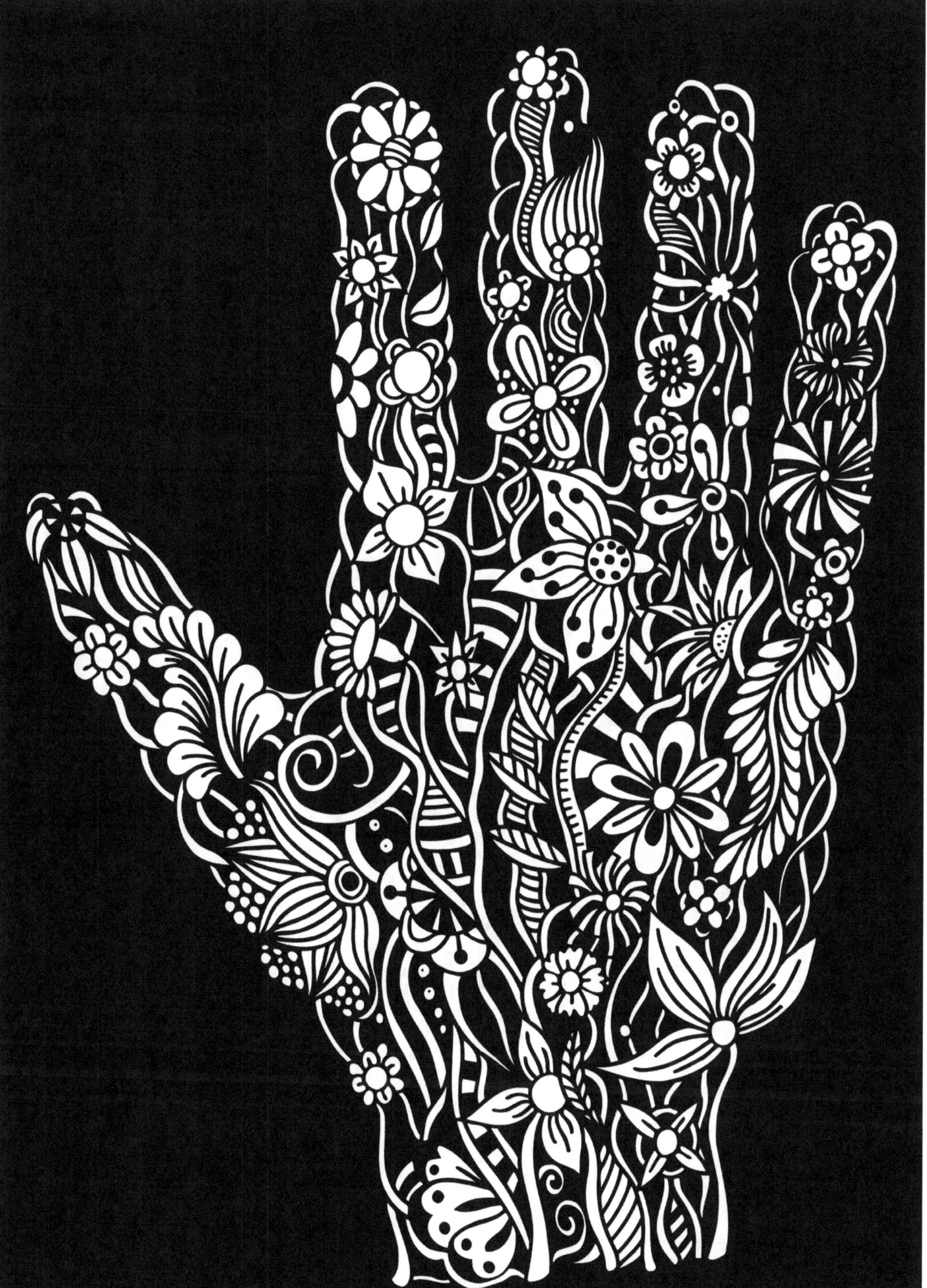